DESIGN
Idea Book

by Karen Templer

Oxmoor House

SUNSET BOOKS

Vice President, General Manager: Richard A. Smeby
Vice President, Editorial Director: Bob Doyle
Director of Operations: Rosann Sutherland
Marketing Manager: Linda Barker
Art Director: Vasken Guiragossian
Special Sales: Brad Moses

Senior Editor: Carrie Dodson Davis
Designer: David Bullen
Copy Editor: Katherine Boller
Proofreader: Denise Griffiths
Prepress Coordinator: Danielle Johnson
Production Specialist: Linda M. Bouchard

Cover photograph by Tria Giovan; details on page 222.

For their help in making this book a possibility,
we would like to extend special thanks to
Abigail Banks, Leighton Batte, Derick Belden,
Kimberley Burch, Karen Carroll, Maelynn Cheung,
Mary Kay Culpepper, Karen Downs, John Floyd,
Kay Fuston, Holly Goff, Eleanor Griffin, Jean Herr,
Melissa Hoover, Larry Hunter, Claire LeBlanc,
Kenner Patton, Keri Payne, Susan Payne, Laurl Self,
Bill Stephens, Katie Tamony, and Spencer Toy.

10 9 8 7 6 5 4 3 2
First printing June 2007

ISBN-13: 978-0-8487-3196-0
ISBN-10: 0-8487-3196-4
Library of Congress Control Number: 2007924938.
Printed in the United States of America.

For additional copies of the *Design Idea Book*
or any other Sunset book,
visit us at www.sunsetbooks.com
or call 1-800-526-5111.

contents

steal these ideas!

EVERY YEAR a number of the country's top magazines team up with the best architects and designers in the business to create designer showhouses, or "idea houses." The purpose is to create homes that are not just beautiful but innovative—making use of the latest technologies and materials, addressing the way we live in our homes today, and putting every square foot of space to work.

In this book, you'll find the best of the best: rooms and ideas from nearly forty houses from magazines as diverse as *Sunset, Southern Accents, Cooking Light, Coastal Living, Southern Living,* and *Cottage Living.* The homes run the design gamut, range from a 280-square-foot garage apartment to a 12,000-square-foot mansion, and include both new construction and renovations. In addition to a detailed tour of rooms for living, dining, sleeping, cooking, working, and playing, we'll show you how they did it—from the flooring to the ceilings, and everything in between. So if you're building, renovating, or simply looking for ways to make your space more livable—doing it yourself or working with a designer—you'll find a wealth of thinking you can learn from, and ideas you can use.

how we live now

Home life is different than it was just a few decades ago, with everything now moving at a faster pace. Largely gone are the days of single-income households and full-time help for middle-class families — more of us are working than ever before (with an increasing percentage working at home) while also trying to run our households, spend time with our loved ones, and set foot outside when possible. Computers are as common as televisions, and technology has had an impact on nearly every household function. Plus it's a more casual world we live in. Our houses have had to adapt.

The kitchen island is now the hub of the home. En suite bathrooms are making private spaces ever more private, while open-plan living spaces put more of the family in the same room at once. Home offices take myriad forms. Laundry rooms are evolving into mixed-use utility rooms, accommodating anything from gift-wrapping to dog-washing. And once-regional features such as mudrooms and screened porches are cropping up all over, because they make a house more livable.

But even as our homes grow and change with shifting concerns, the age-old challenge remains: How do you create a home that will reflect both your taste and your lifestyle? Let these designers show you the way.

A ROOM FOR LIVING Casual elegance, an open floor plan, integration of technology, and a connection to the outdoors epitomize today's attitudes toward the making of a home. The red of this kitchen island emphasizes its starring role in the modern household.

entryways & landings

What does your front hall or foyer say about your house? It's the first impression anyone will have of your home, and yet it's an easy space to neglect when building or decorating.

A good entryway eases the transition from outdoors to in—setting a stylistic tone for the interior while also offering a spot to drop your keys and umbrella. Likewise, stair landings and hallways needn't be simply for passing through. A narrow hall can make a great display space for artwork or a collection; a wide landing might be the perfect reading nook. Make the most of these spaces and your home will feel both larger and more welcoming.

The entryways and landings on the following pages were designed with as much consideration as any other room in the house. They include everything from a formal foyer to an intimate entry hall to a tackle room, and every one of them offers ideas for instantly transmitting the essence of a home, whatever it may be.

ROOM TO LINGER The second-floor landing of this elegant beach house provides access to a large balcony but is a compelling space all on its own. Floor-to-ceiling sheers, patterned with chenille dots, filter the sunlight; the light, in turn, makes an art piece of the drapes. Stools and a small chair provide occasional seating, a paneled niche in the long wall is an alluring backdrop for a painting, and the natural fiber runner—cut to follow the shape of the space—is a textural foil for the glossy grey of the domed ceiling.

THE HALLWAY REDEFINED Forming a T just before the living room, then spanning the entire width of this North Carolina mountain retreat, this high-functioning hallway houses seating, storage, artwork, and even a wet bar (above) along the way. A dark chocolate wash on the walls, wainscoting, columns, and banister contributes to the warm, intimate feel of the space— in striking contrast to the loftiness of the living room beyond.

Upstairs, an oversize landing is furnished with
a pair of deep armchairs and a massive cabinet.
Looking out onto the soaring living room, the space
provides a fun vantage point for party guests. It
also serves as a sitting room for those staying in the
second-floor bedrooms.

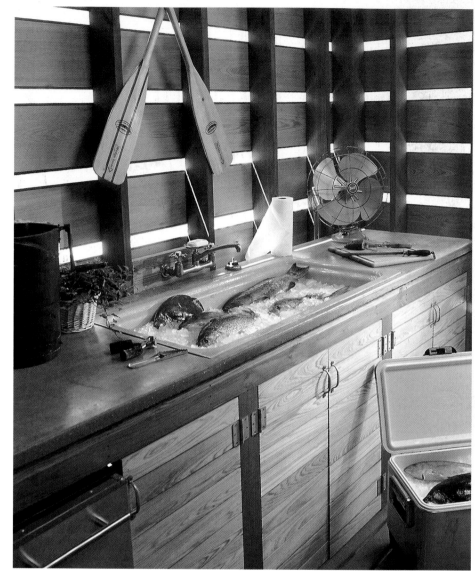

THE PURPOSE-DRIVEN ENTRY The vestibule at the front entrance of this Florida river home is designed not as a formal entryway but as a tackle room—declaring the home a fishing camp from the moment one steps inside. In addition to abundant hooks and cubbies for handy storage of everyone's gear, the space is equipped with a sink and counter for cleaning the day's catch, and a mini-fridge for bait and beer. The gaps between the horizontal slats lend a unique look to the space and let light in, but they're fitted with screens to keep mosquitoes out.

The design of the interior paneling and stair rail reflects the slat treatment of the exterior and entryway. A wide spot in the upstairs hallway, just outside the children's room, is fitted with basic built-in bookshelves and stocked with toys. The result is ready play space out of the grown-ups' way.

ENTERING AN OTHERWORLD The front door of this 1920s home originally opened into a small vestibule. One of the most dramatic features of the renovation is the two-story hall that vestibule now opens into, with its stunning, cypress-clad stairs. The large lantern, weathered statue, and pots of moss—sitting on bare, antique floorboards—give the space an almost otherworldly quality. From the front door, one looks directly down the hallway, with storage closets on the left and a laundry room on the right, all with doors of the same cypress used for the stairs and the coat closet. The hall terminates in a cypress-paneled library that separates the master suite from this passageway.

REFLECTING A SETTING This foyer deftly reflects both the home's architecture and its Chesapeake Bay environs. A narrow, Craftsman-style door, flanked by landscape paintings, makes a virtue of the powder room, while white risers and honey-stained stair treads lead the eye to the larger painting and shorebird sculpture at the turn in the stairs. The space above the powder room was left open for display, contributing to the airy feel. The second-floor landing is used to full effect, offering an out-of-the-way reading spot with built-in bookshelves and storage. Reclaimed heart-pine flooring gives the new house a sense of history, as do the vintage maps on the walls.

A BEACH-FANCY WELCOME

The refined island style of this Florida house is encapsulated in its foyer, where a shell-encrusted mirror and louvered wainscoting—as well as the bright seahorse painting in the small hallway to the left—are beachy counterpoints to the beaded chandelier, coffered ceiling, hand-painted cabinet, and double doorway topped with an arch and pickets.

Ventilation being paramount in tropical settings, louvers are a popular feature in island architecture. While the louvers on the door-height wainscoting in the foyer (opposite) are strictly for looks, functional louvers appear throughout the home in a variety of locations. Among these are the kitchen cabinets, balcony railing, closet doors, and the double doors of the great-room entrance.

INVITING THE OUTDOORS IN Designed for an "environmentally sensitive master-planned community," this home is built of local stone that carries into its foyer, literally bringing the outdoors in. The rustic furnishings, local art, and mesquite flooring also help tie the house to its Texas setting. The foyer opens onto a long hallway lined with French doors that lead to a covered terrace.

A GRAND FOYER THE COASTAL WAY A skirted table, welcoming armchair, and wall of built-in shelving make the entry to this coastal home feel grand, but the details—nautical stripes, a shell collection, locally made baskets, rattan combined with plush upholstery—immediately establish a casual tone. Whitewashed pine paneling, inset with a large porthole window, lends a sun-bleached effect.

AN ELEGANT PROGRESSION

This brief hallway acts as an intimate foyer before opening into a grand, two-story stair-well, drawing one into and through the space. A Regency bench and softly patterned rug are practical and inviting. An arched ceiling and glossy trim add to the refinement. Just inside the front door is a small study; pocket doors allow for a wide doorway. To the right of the bench is a powder room.

INVITINGLY ORNATE Taking cues from its Spanish-Moorish exterior, this Southern California home boasts an ornate doorway and terra-cotta tiles that lead up the walk, into the entry, and right back out again to the pool and patio. The living room is situated to the side, set off by a deep, arched doorway and a shift from the terra cotta to hardwood.

heart of the home

Over the past couple of decades, a host of factors have caused a shift in how our homes look and work. Our increasingly casual lifestyle has made formal living and dining rooms less common; kitchens are getting bigger since that's where we now do our living and our entertaining—doing the cooking ourselves; and the rise of the loft aesthetic has led to the popularity of the open-floor-plan home, with little or no division between the kitchen and the other rooms. A larger house might still have a formal living room and dining room along with a kitchen that's reminiscent of the early settlers' "keeping room"—one large room meant for living, cooking, eating, and whatever else might arise.

Like all changes, these present new challenges. The "formal" rooms you'll see in these homes are more casual than they would have been in the past, marrying elegant furnishings with fabrics that are meant to be sat on. And having the kitchen in the living room—or vice versa—means giving new thought to what the kitchen looks like, as well as how it manages a mess. The designers of these spaces finesse all of that, and much more.

MODEST GRANDEUR When renovating and greatly expanding this 1920s Tudor, architect-designer Bill Ingram "didn't want it to seem grandiose," but a subtle English influence and superlative attention to detail are apparent throughout. In the breakfast room, a settee nestles between a pair of built-in cabinets, and a slender drop-leaf table can seat six for informal meals. The elegant floor is actually quite humble—concrete tiles inlaid with hardwood planks—but it and the trio of windows, embellished with transferware platters, give the small space an undeniable grandness.

In the living room, cypress paneling, ceiling beams, reclaimed oak flooring, and a gently worn rug give the renovated house a sense of age. The cypress repeats as the lining of a niche, setting off the artwork displayed there. The sofa and chairs are all traditional shapes upholstered in a mix of creamy neutrals, allowing details such as the cypress, the sideboard's rippled doors, and the quartet of framed fish-eye mirrors to be the stars of the space. The deep doorway to the right of the niche leads through the pantry to the kitchen and breakfast room, which circles back to the dining room.

The dining room's spare furnishings, unadorned windows, and candle-laden chandelier evoke an Old World dining hall. Ingram paid particular interest to the windows in the house. Some, like the one to the left of the dining table, are set deeply into the wall. All were made to look leaded. He simply specified windows with many small panes, then painted the trim inside and out to get the effect he wanted.

Old meets new in the kitchen, where there is no shortage of modern conveniences. A gleaming stove, pasta boiler, and stainless countertop are set into a hearth-like alcove capped with a rustic beam. Ivory tiles form the backsplash, and the transferware plates match those in the breakfast room. A second beam is set into the wall over the double ovens. Ingram designed the stunning island—chestnut with a granite top—which looks like it could have come straight from the mead hall. Its round shape and the upholstered stools make it the perfect cross between an island and a table.

BRIGHT AND COZY Since the living room of this Hamptons cottage opens to the outdoors, designer Steven Gambrel borrowed his color scheme from the pool and sky. Painted or mirrored furniture works with the wall and trim colors—all whites, blues, and silvery greys—to keep the room light and airy, while darker paint on the doors provides contrast and disguises wear. Upholstery is kept to durable, neutral solids and ticking stripes, with color and pattern reserved for more unexpected spots: the geometric-print canvas floorcloth and striped curtain edging. A pair of doors and a pass-through tie the living room to the kitchen and breakfast room but leave enough wall space for ample storage and counters.

Painted cabinetry, stainless appliances, and soapstone countertops continue the living room's color scheme, as do small appliances that repeat the orange of its floorcloth. A dozen industrial light fixtures march across the glossy white ceiling, which reflects the daylight allowed in by bare windows at one end and sheer roman shades at the other. The pedestal table, banquette (actually two pieces side by side), and painted rattan chairs function as a breakfast spot, extra workspace, or a place for party guests to gather without getting in the cook's way. Here the color and stripes begin to take a bolder stance, though kept in check by the wood table.

Down a short hallway from the living room, the family room gets an added dose of coziness from its small scale and enriched version of the color scheme. Here a brown corduroy sofa keeps company with a pair of eggplant armchairs. As in the other rooms, contrast piping on the furniture accentuates the shapes. Additional interest comes from the striped window coverings (matching curtains and roman shades, with the stripe on the horizontal), orange trim, oversize lamps, and drum-shaped end tables upholstered in orange leather with nailheads. Upholstered floor screens hung with artwork are an upscale take on corkboards.

THE NEW GREAT ROOM An inverted floor plan puts this great room on the second floor, where its long wall of windows overlooks the Gulf of Mexico. The open room is divided into distinct kitchen, dining, and living zones by a pair of chest-high cabinets, which also provide storage. One backs up to the kitchen counter (and has been tiled on that side as a back-splash); the second floats between the dining table and the living space, and has doors on both sides. With the contemporary styling of its dark wood cabinetry, and a giant gilt-framed mirror over the stove, the kitchen is as chic as any living room. A pair of niches (not shown) houses the refrigerator, a bar, and extra cabinetry, allowing for the minimalist look of the kitchen itself.

The dining and living spaces feature contemporary furniture in a mix of styles; the color scheme is an expert mix of warm and cool tones. Perhaps the room's most striking feature is the treatment of the windows, which run along three walls, extend all the way to the floor (except in the kitchen), and provide access to the balcony. Hung from a continuous iron rail, the sunny, yellow-checked drapery is an inventive cross between café curtains and wainscoting. Not only does it make for a unique look, but the horizontality of this treatment balances out the height of the room, with its peaked, timbered ceiling. Equally creative are the sconces mounted at intervals along the curtain rail.

OLD WORLD CHIC The architect and the interior designer of this European-eclectic house agreed the wall of windows planned for the living room, which would afford an expansive view of the house next door, was not the best solution. So they devised a trio of alcoves instead, two of which were fitted with built-in bookshelves and high, round, semi-opaque windows. Now the wall is home to books, art, and a settee, and the room enjoys light and privacy both. To keep the large room from seeming cavernous, all of the furniture is over-size—from the 102-inch-wide sofa to the deep armchairs and generous sideboard. Lamps, candlesticks, and artwork are used in multiples. The narrow passage to the hallway and the adjacent nine-foot opening into the dining room are arched like the alcoves.

The aura of Old World comfort continues in the dining room, where designer Mary Evelyn McKee kept things simple yet sophisticated. A duo of ornate, straight-backed chairs, upholstered in crewelwork, can be pulled in when needed and add interest to the straightforward arrangement of round table and linen-skirted chairs. The room's focal point is not the chandelier, as is often the case, but the window treatment. Ivory over a charcoal stripe, with a charcoal ribbon dividing the two, the curtains are so heavily gathered that McKee likens them to "billowing ball-gown skirts."

While the rest of the house evokes a European villa, the kitchen is unapologetically contemporary, which the designer says is a European approach. "You will often see European houses remodeled in this way, with high-tech, modern kitchens worked into centuries-old rooms." But the kitchen still feels very much of this house because the ceiling, flooring, and high, round windows carry in from the living room. Opting not to make it an eat-in kitchen, McKee was able to furnish it with a large stainless island and copious cabinetry. Overhead is a mix of open shelving, slatted doors, and an organizational rail system. There is also room for a double oven (not shown) set into the wall next to the refrigerator, multiple sinks, deep drawers, and a wine fridge.

PRACTICAL ELEGANCE In this beachfront home, elegance and practicality are equal partners. For example, some of the living room's throw pillows are covered in mother-of-pearl buttons, but the wing chair that sits in front of the French doors is covered in an outdoor fabric, albeit in ivory. While it feels like a "formal" living room, it is open to the kitchen and is separated from the dining room by just a pair of Craftsman-style columns and a built-in buffet topped with a model ship.

The elegant-and-practical principle carries through in the dining room, where a glass chandelier and wall of mirrors share space with a built-in bar—complete with temperature-controlled wine fridge—that cuts down on the need for trips to the kitchen. Likewise, the button-tufted settee looks glamorous with the Queen Anne–style table, but its leather upholstery stands up to spills. The combination of bamboo blinds and fringed drapes allows for total control of light and privacy.

Warm wood tones and ivory continue to predominate in the kitchen, with gleaming countertops and slate backsplashes providing the dash of elegance required to keep up with the adjacent living room. Here the bamboo blinds stand alone, and the designers opted for a mix of finishes on the cabinetry—both to break up the expanse and to make the new room feel as if it has had time to evolve. Modern touches include acrylic-front bin drawers and stainless appliances: not just range and refrigerator but warming drawer, microwave, and dishwasher. Just off the kitchen is a walk-through pantry.

A SWEDISH-FORMAL FARMHOUSE Keeping in the style of traditional farmhouses, the front door of this rural Virginia home opens directly into the living room, and yet it's a formal living room in a decidedly upscale farmhouse. Here and in the formal dining room, pale colors and painted finishes establish a subtly Swedish tone that is carried throughout the home's main rooms. Chairs and sofas—all new but in classic shapes—are upholstered in unpretentious cotton fabrics, and windows are likewise dressed. In the dining room, paneled walls were hand-painted with branches and native songbirds, giving an effect that designer David H. Mitchell says is "like a slightly folksy version of formal scenic wallpaper."

In the eat-in kitchen, the cabinetry's Old World hardware and distressed painted finish reinforce the Swedish farmhouse motif; Mitchell floated some of the cabinets "so they look like they were added over time." The countertops are a mix of surfaces to suit a variety of tasks: butcher block on the island, stainless steel beside the stove, and honed granite everywhere else. All are complemented by the granite tile backsplashes. The seating space along one side of the island accommodates breakfasts and snacks while the trestle table is large enough for family dinners. A sideboard and wide window seat round out the simple furnishings. Matching chandeliers hang over the island and table.

The adjacent family room, with its peaked ceiling, is perfectly square, lending itself to a symmetrical arrangement. Mitchell mixes it up, though, by mispairing the chairs and varying the side tables. The fireplace on one side of the room and television on the other are equally weighted in this layout. Situated between the terrace and garden—French doors on either side lead the way—the room has a flagstone floor; it's warmed by a striped wool rug.

BLUE-RIDGE BEAUTY Just about everything in this house is geared toward capitalizing on its breathtaking views of the Blue Ridge Mountains, but nowhere more so than the 20-foot-high bay of windows in the living room. Broad as well as tall, the room easily accommodates multiple intimately scaled seating areas, which orbit a round ottoman centered under the outsize chandelier. The pale rug and furnishings are balanced by the stone fireplace, chocolate walls, and dark wood paneling. The furniture is a cosmopolitan mix of antiques, upholstered pieces, and contemporary wicker. Since the windows and their dressing are inherently dramatic, given their scale, a plain fabric was used for the curtains; they lend the room a golden glow.

Through the wide archway in the living room is a comparatively snug dining room. Directly across the hallway is the kitchen. The home's Arts and Crafts architecture is apparent in the narrow cabinets built into the hallway's arches, and it is reinforced by the Stickley chairs and benches around the dining table. A trio of lanterns, in place of a chandelier, hit the same rustic note as the mantel does in the living room. Using a pear print in the home's autumnal color scheme, Phillip Sides designed an upholstered wainscoting for the dining space and used the same fabric for a boxed treatment on the kitchen windows. Behind the stove, steel tiles are an unexpected touch.

Next to the kitchen is a "garden room" that extends the kitchen's functionality and serves myriad purposes. With a door nearer the garage and breezeway than the formal entrance, it's the de facto front door for residents. It houses an undercounter washer and dryer (not shown), a deep farmhouse sink, and a powder room. The table, with its charming tractor-seat stools, is equally attractive as a breakfast spot or work table; that and the robin's-egg cabinets, dramatic plaid drapery, and refined light fixture elevate it well beyond any mere utility room.

ECO-FABULOUS Walnut-stained maple cabinetry helps set the tone in this house, which was designed by Laura Britt to be Earth-friendly and energy-efficient, and to bring a sense of the outdoors in. With both an island and a peninsula—the counter of which extends outward on the living room side to form a bar—the kitchen makes maximal use of its 175 square feet. Glass doors on the island cabinets and the upper extensions make serving pieces easy to locate. The iridescent mosaic tiles of the backsplash are recycled glass. At the breakfast end of the room, a matching cabinet becomes a built-in buffet.

The living room (below) is open
to the kitchen and continues the
cabinetry, but the dining room strikes
a slightly more formal note. The fireplace is constructed of local stone;
the comfortable, upholstered chairs
are sophisticated cousins to those in
the breakfast room; recessed lighting,
a contemporary pendant fixture, and
a coconut-shell-crusted floor lamp
provide a mix of light. The picture
windows look onto the garden and
are treated with a coating to minimize
heat and glare.

A GRACIOUS ECONOMY This modestly proportioned Georgia beach house shows influences both Southern and Caribbean. The great room is literally the heart of the symmetrical home: The loft directly above it contains a sitting room (far right); doors on either side of the dining area lead to the two bedrooms; the porthole window over the stove looks into the stairwell, accessed by the door to the left of the kitchen; and the door to the kitchen's right leads into a function-packed utility room (page 90). The 25-foot ceiling—painted the traditional porch-ceiling blue—combines with three walls of sliding glass to blur the distinction between indoors and out.

The deep espresso stain on the island—with massive posts copied from a British Colonial bed—not only demarcates the kitchen from the dining room, but sets it apart visually from the cabinetry, making it feel more like a stately piece of furniture. Because the adjacent pantry handles the dirty work, the kitchen cabinets are free to look and function like a pair of old-fashioned built-in buffets. The custom-cut front for the stove alcove is both glamorous and whimsical, casting a wave-shaped shadow onto the stainless surround.

FRENCH-COUNTRY REFINEMENT Designer Cathy Kincaid treated the spacious kitchen of this Dallas mansion as a "keeping room"—an old-fashioned mixed-use space—and loaded it with French-country charm. The double refrigerators are fronted to match the cabinetry, which is painted a soft green, allowing the massive Wolf range, with its black hood and creamy subway tile backsplash, to be the focal point of the kitchen area. Exposed rafters and antique plank flooring add a touch of earthiness.

Low, upholstered armchairs and a matching ottoman (pulled up to a fireplace with imported limestone mantel), toile curtains along the arcade, and decoratively painted lanterns and chairs all continue the design theme and the red-and-green color scheme. Storage units beside the fireplace were designed to look like antique cabinets recessed into the walls, complete with curtain-lined glass doors.

MIXED AND MATCHED This great room, which encompasses the living and dining rooms, takes advantage of its dunes-and-water view with unimpeded bay windows and glass doors. The kitchen looks through the space across its L-shaped counter bar, and it mimics the sand and surf with its pearlescent quartz countertops and shimmering blue tile walls. The casual vibe, mix of wood tones and finishes, and exposed ceilings carry throughout the space.

CRAFTSMAN LIGHTENS UP With its parchment-colored paint in place of traditional stains, and daylight streaming in through cabinets with glass doors on both sides, this Orange County kitchen might be described as the lighter side of Craftsman. A leaded-glass door, glass-front drawers, and tile mosaics provide points of interest around the space, while stone and wood countertops accommodate differing uses. Matching cabinetry in the breakfast room is painted a dark green to look like a piece of custom furniture. A pass-through keeps the space from being completely closed off from the living room.

utility spaces

When a designer tackles a home, every room counts, and that includes what many of us would think of as the mundane spaces—mudrooms, laundry rooms, workspaces of all kinds. In any utility room, good design means good functionality. Everything needs a place. And that's what you'll see here: from a shipshape pantry to a clever pet-grooming station. But these rooms also demonstrate that every space you spend time in deserves to be as attractive as it is useful.

If your family's primary entrance is the rear or garage door, fashion a mudroom that's as well-considered as the front hall. If you're a gardener, make a potting room as pleasing as any home office. And if it's a laundry room or wet bar you're devising, create a space as well-designed as the washing machine or wine fridge you'll fit it with. Not only will your home function better, but chores will feel less like chores when you've got a beautiful room in which to perform them.

THE ULTIMATE PANTRY This galley-style utility room, tucked discreetly but conveniently off the kitchen end of a mixed-use great room, is as hard-working as a space can be. Opposite a wall housing a refrigerator, storage cabinets, a washer and dryer, and an extra sink (see page 78) is the ultimate compact butler's pantry. The lower cabinets on this wall share space with pull-out baskets and a wine fridge. Above them, open shelving and bottle racks keep glassware, dishes, and a selection of wines at the ready. An uninterrupted prep counter provides ample workspace and keeps the mess out of view of the great room.

A ROOM FOR ALL USES This long, narrow area alongside the kitchen and family room has been converted into a multipurpose space that facilitates everything from crafts to laundry to paying bills. A corkboard over the craft area hangs on a sliding track and is finished on the other side to resemble a barn door; it can be slid in front of the kitchen pass-through to close it off. A supply cart on casters doubles as extra counter space when needed.

All of the cabinetry in the multipurpose room matches that in the kitchen (previous page), but here a wood counter becomes a desktop, and a sink serves a range of needs, including laundry. The wall-mounted television keeps one company while doing chores.

DRINKS ALL AROUND The kitchen of this Texas home is separated from the living-dining room by a spacious wet bar and wine room. With a refrigerator, sink, ice-maker, and cabinets full of glassware and other supplies, the space is a boon while entertaining: Guests can help themselves to drinks and finger foods set up in the bar area rather than encroaching on the kitchen. River rock tile floors help keep the room cool, and pocket doors allow it to be closed off when desired.

THE BEAUTY OF UTILITY There's no reason a utility room can't be as beautiful as any other room in the house. This pantry/mudroom (opposite), which connects the home's living room to both kitchen and screened porch, has the same floors, cabinetry, and windows as the kitchen. The granite counters match that of the kitchen island. The same cabinetry and windows show up again on the other side of the house, in the laundry room, which has the same hardwood flooring as the hallway and library it abuts. In addition to the wall shown, there are two walls of cabinetry and closets for multiple kinds of storage.

BETTER THAN A BUTLER A classic butler's pantry, such as the one in this gracious Louisiana home, bridges the kitchen and dining room and organizes everything needed for entertaining—from serving pieces and silver to table linens. This one also boasts an undercounter fridge, fronted with the same reclaimed cypress as the rest of the cabinetry. Brass grillwork in the overhead cabinet doors and a small chandelier over the sink add French-country character.

BEYOND THE LAUNDRY A state-of-the-art washer and dryer, overhead cabinets, a mosaic tile backsplash, and ample counter space make this a dream of a laundry room. An extra wall of cabinetry and a peninsula take it further, making it a space for projects of all sorts. The farmhouse sink is deep enough to accommodate potting chores, and the stone floors and countertops can handle any mess—and look beautiful doing it.

EVERYTHING IN ITS PLACE This sizable room off the garage is equal parts mudroom, laundry room, and all-purpose project space. With cabinetry, open shelving, pull-out baskets, hooks, and bins, there is truly a place for everything, while a large center island offers plenty of room to spread out. The mix of solid and woven doors, the mosaic tile back-splash, and bright glass tiles laid into the limestone floor make the room as engaging as it is functional.

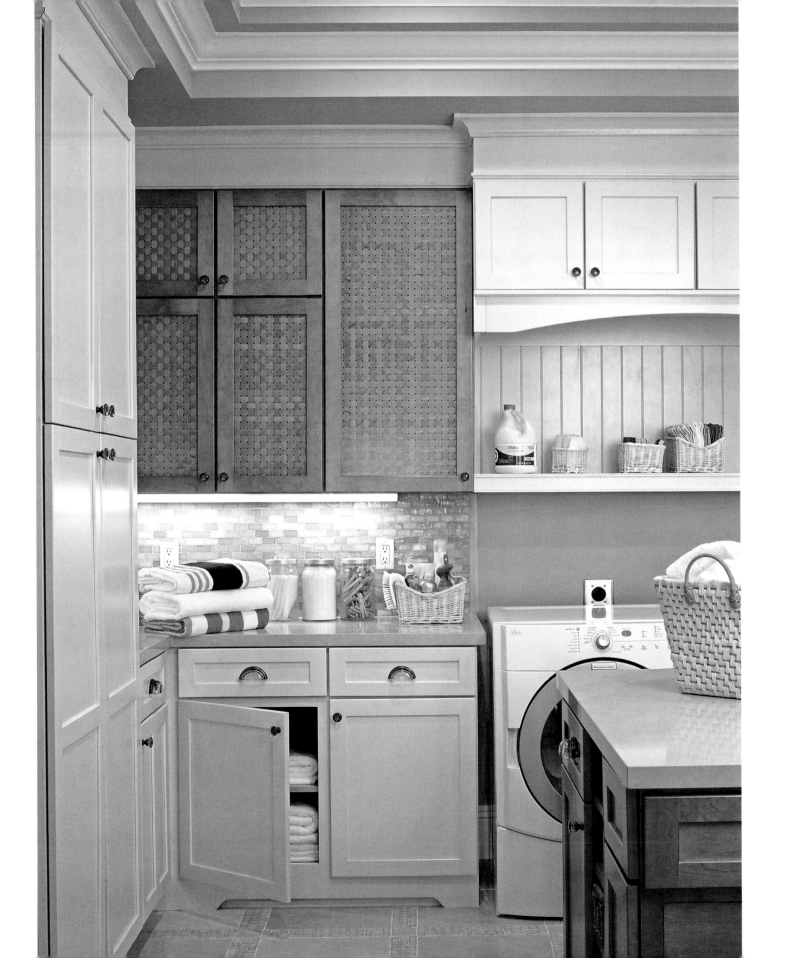

KEEPING IT HANDY Designer Steven Gambrel doesn't believe in hiding away the stuff of everyday life. Accordingly, inside the back door, the mudroom hosts a long row of coat pegs, an overhead shelf, a bench for donning or removing one's rain boots, and room underneath to store them. In the adjacent laundry room, open shelving keeps such necessities as paper towels and cleaning supplies handy—even the litter box is where the cat can easily find it. By contrast, an extra-wide, old-fashioned porcelain sink is a beautiful alternative to the standard molded utility sink.

ONE FOR THE DOGS Just off the "friends' entrance"—an informal second entrance common to Southern homes—and also opening to the garden, this laundry room and adjacent mudroom were designed with the family dog in mind. Described by the designer as a "pet hotel," the mudroom features a doggie door, food dish, automatic water bowl, and a stall shower that's useful for human and canine alike. Continuous tile surfaces eliminate the need for a shower door, making it easier to bathe Fido. The gilt-framed dog portrait over the laundry room sink adds a touch of whimsy.

POTTING ROOM DELUXE

This workroom/potting room at the rear of the garage has a narrow sink with double faucets set into a poured concrete counter, which was stained green and given a rock-face edge. A small fridge doubles as a cooler for cut flowers. Painted tongue-and-groove paneling makes the space feel fresh and tidy but also resists mildew.

AT THE READY In this combination laundry and potting room, a swiveling cabinet door is hung with hooks for organizing hand tools.

A SIMPLE PLAN A potting room can be as simple as a small shed or corner of the garage, as this one is, as long as there's a nearby water source. The most important feature is a counter at a comfortable height for performing the otherwise back-straining task.

work & play

These days we demand more from our homes than just a place to make a meal, sleep, and take a bath. We need home offices, playrooms (for kids and adults alike), and quiet retreats from our hectic lives. If you have the luxury of an empty bedroom, a basement, or a nook under the eaves, will you make a library, an exercise room, or a tiki lounge? With a little ingenuity, anything is possible.

There's plenty of ingenuity on display in the rooms you're about to see—from the wine cellar to the attic playloft. Like utility rooms, these are rooms that take heavy cues from the purposes they serve, but these are designed as destinations—be it a study where a kid can really concentrate or a game room that prolongs the life of any party.

COMMAND CENTRAL This home-organization nook occupies a small room just inside the back door that might otherwise have been designed as a mudroom. Instead, it accommodates a bulletin board, vintage office chair, and family computer, and offers convenient open storage of otherwise stray belongings. Designer Tim Schelfe points out that the distressed finish of the cabinetry, the slate floors, and the solid-surface countertop "set the stage for heavy use and high traffic."

SURF LOUNGE EXTRAORDINAIRE This California Craftsman hides a surprise in its basement: a groovy surf-style lounge and game room designed by Steve Jones, of Quiksilver surf goods fame. All the old standards are here— mid-century seating, a pool table and bar, retro posters and seascape paintings—but details such as the thatched ceiling, built-in aquarium, and pendant lights made from Japanese fishing floats kick it up a notch.

WHERE GROWN-UPS PLAY This home features a pair of sophisticated playrooms for grown-ups: a billiards room on the second floor and a wine cellar in the basement. Both are filled with the sort of plush furniture that encourages one to relax and stay awhile—velvet in the billiards room, leather in the wine cellar. With its dark ceiling, sloping walls (upholstered in the same crimson print as one of the chairs), and mahogany pool table, the upstairs room has an old-fashioned gentlemen's club feel to it. A television and a small bar round out the offerings. In the cellar, dramatic architecture and accessories—such as the sprawling chandelier—are an elegant backdrop for private wine tastings or dinner-and-cigars parties.

A STIMULATING STUDIO Built into the space over the garage, this is a play loft for kids of all ages. Geared toward the fun and creativity of arts and crafts, it was treated to a full paintbox of colors—all in a gloss finish for easy cleanup. The sink is a must and is surrounded by plenty of storage space. The oversize daybed, upholstered in rugged outdoor fabrics, is a great place to read or nap, while the presence of a full bathroom means it can double as a guest bed.

GAME FOR A CROWD Just off the upstairs landing, under the roofline, an undesignated space in the floor plan was turned into a lounge and game room with a slightly global flavor. Anchored by a cocoa-colored sofa that runs the full width of the room, the space is home to multiple seating areas and an old-fashioned game table. Because the sofa is pushed up against the windows, soft roman shades were employed. The designer didn't let the sloping walls stop him from hanging artwork and sconces on the lower parts—that and the sofa make the whole room feel pleasantly low-slung.

A CLASSIC READING ROOM Chocolate leather upholstery with brass nailheads, set into white oak paneling instead of traditional mahogany, is a fresh and contemporary take on library style. But it is every bit warm and inviting. A buffet hides miscellany so that the room is all books and suitably plush furniture for curling up with them.

TO ESCAPE THE SUN A small room on the non-beach side of this house was designed as a retreat from all the sun and surf. The lacquered paneling on the walls and ceiling gives the room a retro flavor, which is reinforced by the furnishings and the geometric print fabric. Used on the fronts of the media shelving, the fabric was also stretched and framed for wall hangings in the same dimensions as the windows. Hung on slide rails, they can be used to black out the windows, either for watching movies or when the room doubles as sleeping quarters for guests.

More and more people are content to have a television out in the open, especially in a dedicated space like the media room opposite. But in a more formal room there's often still a desire to store or disguise it in some fashion. Our showhouse designers demonstrated a variety of ways to do so. Among those are a steel vault over the fireplace, a cabinet with sliding doors, and a recess above the mantel covered with a mirror that becomes translucent when the television illuminates it from behind.

A STUDY IN ELEGANCE Situated right inside the front door and separated from the rest of the house by a soaring stairwell, this room was designed as a classic study. With books, a television, an antique secretary, a number of welcoming chairs, and pocket doors for privacy, the room lends itself to more than just business.

HALLWAY AS HOME OFFICE A desk built into an alcove transforms a second-floor hallway into a surprisingly efficient home office. The alcove is flanked by built-in shelves on one side and a shallow closet, stocked with gift-wrapping supplies, on the other. White paint and a Lucite chair contribute to the airy feel of the space. The wall opposite the desk (not shown) holds additional shelving.

A DESK OF ONE'S OWN With computers getting ever smaller and more portable, a home office can be as simple as an out-of-the-way spot to situate a desk and chair—whether you have a whole room or just a corner of a kitchen, garage, or spare bedroom to work with. Kitchen or workshop cabinetry can be configured to provide as much storage as your job demands. In a second home, a desk and laptop can often mean an extra day or two before you have to head back.

FOR YOUNG SCHOLARS A small, awkward space on the second floor was treated as an old-fashioned study for the children, whose rooms are on either side. Painted a medium blue that shifts with the light, the space was furnished with plush chairs also upholstered in shades of blue—in durable, stain-resistant Ultrasuede. Maps and a globe set a light-heartedly learned tone.

A LEARNING CENTER This second-floor hallway, near the kids' rooms, was transformed into a study area by the addition of built-in cabinetry and a pair of stools. A long bank of cabinet drawers serves as side-by-side desks, with the shelving above dividing it in two. The "cork-boards" are inexpensive grass mats tacked to the walls.

21ST-CENTURY PLAYROOM Furnished with a bright red sectional, distressed media cabinet (with television and video game console), and upholstered ottomans in a mix of colors, a spare bedroom adjacent to the children's rooms becomes an irresistible hangout.

A KID-SIZE HIDEOUT Here the floor plan terminates in a small third-floor space, tucked under the eaves, that's been furnished with scaled-down versions of traditional sitting-room pieces. The addition of the hand-painted trompe l'oeil fireplace, candlesticks, and portrait makes it an imaginative retreat for the kids.

FOR BODY AND SOUL These designers took the concept of workout space a step further, incorporating a small sauna and a meditation and massage room into their floor plans, in what might otherwise have been powder or utility rooms.

AN EXERCISE IN SIMPLICITY A mirrored wall with handrail and some choice pieces of exercise equipment turn this narrow space into a surprisingly elegant workout room. The television helps pass time on the treadmill; a storage bench and floor screen keep odds and ends out of sight.

bed & bath

Whether we're two, twelve, or twenty, it's a big deal the first time we get to decorate our own bedroom. And it never stops being a big deal. A bedroom is a sanctum and it's only natural that each of us wants our room to reflect who we are at a given stage in our lives—and to provide us with what we need when we close the door. For a kid's room, that might mean visual stimulation along with a good table for doing homework; while in a master suite, perhaps it's the tranquility of a canopy bed and a cartoon-free television. And then there is the guest room—the retreat we create for others.

As en suite bathrooms become increasingly common throughout the house, what now sets a master bedroom apart are deluxe amenities such as a fireplace or private balcony—or both. Bathrooms are getting bigger, and are designed to match the bedrooms they adjoin. But the rooms on the following pages are about much more than scale or layout. They're about re-imagining everything from the headboard to the tub surround.

RESORT STYLE ADAPTED A gleaming hardwood floor, minimalist linens, touches of bamboo and coconut shell, and a subtle, tonal color scheme—pale sea-green walls, darker blue-green curtains, and the rich green of the potted plants—make guests in this room feel as if they've checked into a tropical resort. The wide alternating stripes of the curtains are opaque and sheer, for an extra dazzling effect in the bay window.

A POSH RETREAT With its Gulf views, sun-and-sand palette, natural fiber rugs, and judicious mix of wicker and British Colonial furnishings, this master suite is beach chic at its finest. Spots of vibrant yellow are balanced with dark woods and deep blues for a sense of overall calm. In the same vein, both pattern and color are kept to a minimum: The bed is draped with the same modified paisley used for the roman shades, and the yellow stripe of the drapes repeats in the glass lamps. With multiple chairs and a media cabinet, the room offers plenty of options for relaxing.

Between the bedroom and bath is a wide dressing hall, with his-and-her closets, dressers, and upholstered stools. The bathroom is a spa-like space complete with a chaise longue. The room's focal point is the freestanding tub—set into an alcove, on a slab of marble, surrounded by glamorous diamond-shaped tiles, and draped with white sheers. The sunburst mirror reflects the beach view.

THE GETAWAY This master suite, high atop the house, maximizes its vantage point by situating the bed in the middle of the room, looking out over the bay. A half-wall behind the sleigh bed blocks the view of the bathroom without blocking its view outside. The room also offers the homeowners a choice of places to relax: in a plush armchair by the fireplace indoors, or in equally plush wicker chairs on the private balcony.

BRONZED BEAUTY A canopy bed elaborately draped in icy blue silk taffeta gives this master suite a fairy-tale quality, but it's warmed up by the bronze of the giant leaf pattern used on the headboard, curtains, and roman shades. A fireplace and silk rug help to keep the space cozy. The brocade fabric of the bench's throw pillows mimics the antiquing on the mirror behind them.

The bronze tones continue in the bathroom's large terra-cotta tiles, as well as in the hardware on the sconces and pendant fixture, and the frames on the mirrors over the dual vanities. What looks like a many-paned window in the closet door is actually another mirror. The tub is set into an arched alcove but is given an added measure of privacy and intimacy by the upholstered floor screen that encircles it.

A SPLASH OF ORANGE This lofty master bedroom is grounded by its chic, custom-upholstered bed and by unexpected dashes of orange. The headboard and frame are covered in an orange stripe, with the headboard edged in tan leather and pewter nailheads. An ivory wing-back chair is covered—just on the outside—in vivid orange leather. And the armchair and ottoman wear a toned-down orange houndstooth. Used this way, the orange predominates without overpowering all of the soft blues, greys, and tans sharing the space. Likewise, the matching bedside tables with mismatched lamps ever so subtly turn on its ear the expectation of symmetry and harmony in a bedroom, making for a more engaging space. By contrast, the bathroom is all sky and light.

PACKED WITH STYLE For this bedroom, designer Phillip Sides put an iron rail to even more imaginative use than he did in the home's great room (pages 46–49). Suspended from this one are an upholstered "headboard," a channel-quilted throw, and a frameless drawing. The snug room also gets tremendous texture from its grey-and-khaki color scheme, an artful layering of accessories, and, most of all, the oversize botanical-print fabric that's been used for a floor screen, a roman shade, and a wall hanging.

A SHIPSHAPE SUITE The designers of this spare bedroom gave it the look of a ship's cabin by flanking a black, paneled headboard with a pair of shelving towers and hanging three round mirrors above it to suggest portholes. The nautical theme continues with artwork and accessories around the antique secretary. And in the bathroom, vintage water meters—simply mounted to a strip of wood and hung on the wainscoting—stand in for towel hooks.

TO SLEEP IN THE TREES Because this upper-floor bedroom's many windows are shielded by treetops—giving the room a tree-house feel—designer Linda Woodrum was reluctant to drape them, so she draped the bed instead. The neutral color scheme of taupes and tans, combined with crisp white trim, plays up all of the architectural interest in the room: the intricate window frames, wide arch of the seating alcove, horizontal beaded board on walls and ceiling, and the gingerbread detailing at the base of the arch. A ceiling fan keeps the coastal breezes stirring in the room.

A TOUCH OF MINK Upstairs at this house is a room like no other. At the head of twin beds, on chocolate brown walls, the design team mounted floor-to-ceiling silver-leaf frames filled with faux mink. The beds are dressed with fitted bedspreads topped in a softly colored stripe that repeats on the bolsters. Swiss dot wool drapes and a lacquered, tray-topped table provide contrast without competing for the limelight. But the biggest surprise might be the pink ceiling.

bed & bath | 159

SOOTHINGLY BLUE The icy blue walls of this bedroom are warmed up by a handsome canopy bed in bamboo, the dark paisleys of the translucent curtains, and the occasional touch of green. But the blue also gains richness by being layered into the room in different shades—on the door, the desk drawers, the chair and bed, and even the picture frames. The closet door was hung on a sliding rail, allowing room for the striped slipper chair that would otherwise be in its way. A desk gives guests a place to write.

Whether styled like old-fashioned barn doors (top) or given a contemporary twist, doors hung on slide rails are an increasingly popular design trick. Like pocket doors, they eliminate the need for doors to open into a room, so they can be a valuable space-saving device as well as an interesting look. In this entryway (center), which looks directly into the kitchen, a frosted-glass panel can be used to close off the view. When slid in front of the adjacent wall, it becomes an art piece. The wall hangings on slide rails (bottom) double as window coverings.

bed & bath   161

THE PAMPERED GUEST This mountain retreat was designed as a vacation home where as many as three families could peacefully coexist. To that end, it has multiple "master" bedrooms, including this one on the lower level, or guest level. On the scale of a large studio apartment, this room is equal parts sitting room and bedroom, with the bed tucked into a broad niche that can be closed off by curtains. Further delineating the space is a low, custom screen with nailhead detailing. A bench with the same nailhead treatment serves as a coffee table. Echoing its forest setting, the room is dressed in leaf prints, in shades of green and gold.

The suite opens onto a private balcony with mountain views. In the bathroom, a tub is set into a platform of stone tile and surrounded by a gently curving wall of deep green glass tiles that seem perpetually wet. The assemblage is complemented by a blue-green garden stool and iron lantern.

AN ACCOMMODATING SPACE The more space guests have, the more comfortable they'll feel, but that doesn't have to mean anything elaborate. Here a few small pieces of furniture at the foot of the bed—a settee, side chair, and diminutive tables—make the room's occupants feel as if they have their own sitting room. The palette for the space was kept pale and airy for a dreamy effect: a light blue-green on the walls, button-tufted headboard, coverlet, and bed skirt was paired with a single black-and-white print. Ornate touches such as the painted chair and giant sconces—an interesting counterpoint to the petite furnishings—add character to the mix.

The accompanying bathroom was given the same airy effect, with lots of white plus the reflective quality of the mosaic tiles used on the floor and wainscoting. The brass mirror frame harks back to the sconces in the bedroom's sitting area. The toilet gets its own alcove.

A GUEST ROOM WITH A VIEW A cross between sitting room and sleeping quarters, this guest room puts twin beds to creative use. Designed to look like daybeds, they float in the middle of the room, so both offer a view of the landscape across the balcony as well as the television hidden in the Asian-style cabinet. Small, counterpoised tables function as nightstands but are easily relocated so the beds can be pushed together.

Yellow tile in the en suite bathroom makes it feel much sunnier than it actually is. The stone floor and antique-style cabinet and mirror are in keeping with the bedroom's global decor. A small table is always handy near a tub.

UNDER THE EAVES This spare upstairs bedroom, with its neutral palette and twin beds, is equally suitable for children or grown-ups. Rather than avoiding the eaves, the designer situated the brass beds directly under them—with an upholstered bench in between—and conceived a bed-hanging as elegant as any canopy. There's even a lantern descending from behind its ruffle. Each bed has a stool at its foot, and there's still room for a mix of chairs, a chaise, and a whimsical shag ottoman. The armoire houses a television.

BUILT FOR FUN This "guest cottage"—actually a 20- by 14-foot studio apartment above the garage— is a testament to just how much can be accomplished in a small space. The floor plan was left open with the exception of the bathroom, allowing for the bed and bedside tables, a galley-style kitchen with counter bar, and enough seating for the guests to have guests of their own. Susan Lovelace and team filled the space with brightly painted wood, rattan, and wicker furniture—along with funky accents such as the weathered mirror above the sink and the galvanized-tub light fixture over the bar—to give it a cheery, flea-market-chic vibe.

The tongue-and-groove paneling was painted in three shades of aqua, three planks at a time, to create wide but subtle stripes on the walls. Round mirrors appear throughout the space. The fun continues in the bathroom, with its 24-inch, punched-aluminum wall tiles and a sink set into a black vintage-style console table.

SMALL-SPACE INGENUITY In another room-over-the-garage scenario, an even smaller space manages to still offer living, dining, and sleeping arrangements. What makes it possible is the ingenuity of the custom H-shaped room divider, with a sleeper sofa set into one side and shallow settee in the other. A demilune table pulled up to the settee requires less space than a round table would. The leaf print used on the living room's rattan armchairs establishes the all-green color scheme, repeats on throw pillows, and coordinates with the striped window shades. A narrow box fixture hung over the divider adds to the sense of separation.

The bathroom and kitchen–laundry room are separate spaces but continue the striped walls and window coverings from the main room, for a sense of unity. Open shelving in the kitchen solves the problem of having too many doors in a small space, and makes it as easy as possible for guests to find what they need.

KIDS' CAMP This bunk room takes young guests in stride. Brightly colored sleeping bunks are not just fun—they're color-coded. Each bed has a coordinating cubby for kids to stash their beach gear. A niche at the head of each bed is a private place to stash more stuff, and large baskets under the bunks stow toys and other miscellany. The bathroom continues the bright color scheme, but full walls of subway tile and counters of concrete make for easy cleanup.

BEYOND THE EXPECTED A chic palm print in marine blue is unexpected yet right at home in this boy's room, where it's the perfect backdrop for bamboo blinds, a funky rattan chair, and a pair of surfboards—one suspended from the ceiling—in a surf-themed ensemble. In the bathroom, a sea of mixed blue tiles and a retro mirror frame continue the theme, but the bedroom's sophisticated, upholstered walls will easily lend themselves to other uses as the boy grows up or moves on.

LITTLE-GIRL GLAMOUR Tall, draped, twin canopy beds, a sophisticated black-and-white color scheme, and a pair of skirted armchairs in lipstick red add up to a young girl's fantasy of a bedroom. The beds' linen drapes are dressed up with black bell fringe on all sides. The toile window dressings repeat in the bathroom as a shower curtain. A marble tub surround completes the Hollywood-glam look.

A PREPONDERANCE OF PINK This girls' room was decorated the way little girls like to dress—in a riot of colors and patterns, primarily pink. There is button-tufting (on the upholstered headboards), beading (on the box valance), and plenty of ruffles, including two-tiered dust ruffles on the twin beds. The bright yellow table, paired with ladylike chairs, is fit for homework or tea parties. The floor is even painted a glossy pink. Designer David Mitchell uses outdoor fabrics in kids' rooms because they stand up to abuse.

A ROOM TO GROW INTO With its simple lilac-and-orange color scheme, this nursery is designed to age with the girl who grows up in it. In fact, the California poppy painted on one wall is for tracking her height through her early years. Layers of cloth leaves are a creative touch above the window and filter the light emitting from the fixtures they conceal. The window seat lifts up for handy storage of toys and other belongings.

outdoor living

Another shift in how we live today is a new focus on the outdoors. Not only are homes being built or renovated with an eye toward how the interior spaces open to the lawn or garden, but people are finding that creating outdoor rooms is one of the easiest ways to increase their living space. And we're not talking about folding lawn chairs— the new outdoors has all the same comforts and conveniences found inside.

Advances in outdoor fabrics in recent years mean that plushly upholstered furniture is no longer just for the living room. Portable grills are being replaced by fully equipped kitchens. Many homes even boast outdoor showers and sleeping quarters.

On the following pages, you'll find indoor-outdoor porches of every shape, kind, and purpose, and settings as disparate as vintage metal chairs overlooking a patch of green and a lushly furnished loggia with floor-length drapes. All are spaces to make one regret having to ever go inside.

ELEMENTAL COMFORT The spacious sleeping porch off an upstairs bedroom—a traditional feature of Craftsman architecture—is here treated as a sitting room in exemplary indoor-outdoor fashion. Wrought iron and glass are rugged enough to stand up to the weather, but so are the more refined elements—the plush cushions and custom curtains— thanks to advances in outdoor fabrics. Plates hung on the shingled wall add to the living room effect, but there's no mistaking the fresh air and unobstructed view.

THE INSIDE-OUT HOUSE Designed with as much outdoor living space as indoor, this Florida fishing camp features just about every type of outdoor-use space popular today: screened porch, covered sleeping porch, outdoor kitchen, outdoor shower and dressing area, and expansive decks. The fireplace in the second-floor screened porch makes the room suitable for year-round use, and with the rafters and metal roof left exposed, it's an especially pleasant place to hide out from a rainstorm. A pair of daybeds in the corner gives the homeowners the option of sleeping in the fresh air and increases the number of guests the home can accommodate.

On the first floor, a pass-through allows the cook a view of the action on the deck. Built into the base of the chimney, the outdoor kitchen is equipped with a sink, a grill, undercounter storage, and a bar-height counter for serving; barn doors on both sides allow the area to be closed off from inclement weather. The sleeping porch houses three more daybeds. Here the combination of weather-resistant curtains and remote-control retractable screens offers customizable protection against sun, wind, and insects.

Tucked under the other end of the house, a walled dressing
area leads to the outdoor shower under a cistern. Jasmine
vines on a copper-rod trellis provide privacy.

CATCHING A BREEZE The two balconies on this Gulf Coast home host multiple seating arrangements—some for lounging, others for dining, all with a terrific view. The deeper of the two, which spans the front of the house, has roman shades that can be lowered against the sun. Full-length curtains on the waterfront side are made of parachute cloth, both for durability and for the way they ripple in the breeze.

SCREENED LUXURY Screened on three sides, this rear porch provides passage from the living room to the backyard, but along the way it epitomizes the luxury of modern indoor-outdoor living. With its soft rug, curtains, comfortable furnishings, fireplace, and bar, it offers everything the interior rooms do, but with the addition of fresh air and sunshine.

A PORCH WITH PANACHE A wide wraparound porch is the pinnacle of Southern living. This one is home to a table and chairs for outdoor dining as well as deep wicker chairs with colorful striped cushions. The gas fireplace, cozy on cool evenings, backs up to the one in the family room. Candles and greenery dress up the space.

Indoors or out, gas- or wood-burning, functional or decorative, a fireplace makes any space feel more welcoming. It also provides a natural focal point. And when a fireplace is as strikingly designed as those shown here, it requires little in the way of adornment. During warmer months, the mouth of the fireplace makes a great place to display *objets* or cuttings from the garden.

A WELL-APPOINTED PORCH As this screened porch forms a bridge between the main house and its guest room, it serves multiple needs: extending the family's living space while also serving as a separate kitchen and living room for visitors. The galley-style kitchenette has slate tile counters, a large grill, mini-fridge, and prep sink, and looks out over a living-dining area filled with rattan furniture that would be equally at home indoors. All of the fabrics—including the fringe on the throw pillows—are made for outdoor use.

THE NEW OUTDOOR KITCHEN At the rear corner of the lot, a small pool is complemented by a firepit and a screened cabana fitted with the ultimate outdoor kitchen, including a professional-grade grill, draft beer dispenser, stainless counter-height fridge, and even a warming drawer. The hood keeps smoke out of the space while a ceiling fan circulates air, and the floor is the same composite decking used just outside the French doors. Diners have a choice between the wicker table and chairs in the cabana or the teak set with umbrella on the patio. Just beyond the latter, a door leads to a full bathroom with shower, handy for washing off either sand or chlorine before rejoining the party. The crow's nest over the kitchen is accessed via the guest cottage.

THE LUSH LIFE With its cathedral ceiling, clerestory windows, and row of archways framing the view of the grounds, this loggia is all drama. Cathy Kincaid keeps it casual by sticking to the French-country motif established inside; in this case, employing a mix of fabrics—and a tile-topped table—all in the classic provincial color scheme of blue and yellow. Striped curtains, backed with the hot-air balloon print seen on the pillows, soften the stone arches. The fireplace is flanked by alcoves that match the curve of those arches; one is fitted with a storage bench, the other with a small bar, complete with mini-fridge. A blue-striped rug underscores the decor.

NO BOUNDARIES This loggia—with its fireplace, tile "rug" set into the terra cotta, and traditional living room arrangement—doesn't just blur the lines between indoors and out, it obliterates them. The wall that the outdoor room shares with the home's central hallway is constructed entirely of floor-to-ceiling folding glass doors; when they are retracted, the entire first floor is effectively open to the backyard. The addition of an outdoor kitchen means this Southern California family can live outdoors, in style and comfort, nearly year-round.

A STATELY RUSTICITY This stateliest of homes has the sparest of outdoor seating arrangements. Part of the expansion of the home was a wine room (right) tacked onto the rear of the garage. A grotto carved into the back of that addition, just outside the wine room door, is the perfect spot for sipping wine and surveying one's domain. The simple, eclectic mix of vintage pieces—a long bench, two mismatched metal chairs, and a stone-topped table—is every bit as stylish as the home's interior.

DOUBLE THE VIEW This two-story rear porch provides for an elegant terrace on the ground level and a casual sleeping porch above, and takes full advantage of the home's golf course view. Wooden daybeds are perfect for an afternoon nap or overnight guests. Roman shades upstairs and ceiling fans on both levels allow a measure of climate control. The ceilings are also equipped with tiny misters that keep insects at bay.

AN OPPORTUNITY TO LOUNGE When the architect of this home conceived of its curving stone half-walls, topped with columns, it was to tie the front porch in with the rest of the house, where the walls slope gently outward as they reach the ground. The designer saw them as a place to recline and had cushions made to fit, adding to the lounging opportunities already afforded by the rockers and swing.

THE LIVING ROOM AL FRESCO When designing for the outdoors, why not use colors just as vivid as those you'd find in the garden? This covered porch takes exactly the same attitude as the living room that opens onto it (pages 40–41): deep, plushly upholstered furniture, a generously scaled coffee table, low-maintenance rugs, contrast piping for an added punch, and stripes as an accent fabric. The wide bar keeps cocktails and other treats handy for those reluctant ever to leave the porch.

details make the difference

The number of considerations in putting together a room can be daunting, from establishing a style and a color scheme to specifying every last finish, which is why many people run out of steam (or money!) before the job is truly done. The pros understand the scope of it all, weigh critical factors at the outset, and make decisions about things most of us fail to take into account. It's that attention to detail that sets a professionally designed home apart — the commitment to seeing a room all the way through, from the initial flooring selection to the final arrangement of objects on tables and walls.

On the following pages, you'll find guidance on a host of topics — from window treatments and ceilings to creating storage solutions and even carving out extra space in your home.

For every topic you'll see a range of solutions and why each one made sense in its setting. There are more ways to dress a window or a bed than you may have imagined, more issues of scale, texture, and proportion. The better informed you are of your options, the wiser choices you'll make—in keeping with your taste, your budget, and how you intend to use a room. That preparedness means not only that you can fully enjoy the process, but that you'll wind up with better results.

SITTING PRETTY Transforming a blank wall into an inviting sitting area, this simple arrangement is also instructive. A broad table and single, large painting anchor the space. The table's demilune shape allows the button-tufted armchairs to nestle up to it and angle casually toward one another. Warm brown and gold tones balance the cool blue of the chairs, while an ottoman with matching legs but contrasting upholstery stands at the ready.

style

A Dark, bamboo-framed mirrors and wide nautical stripes set a tropical tone in this Florida bathroom, but the designer puts a spin on the motif by rendering the stripes in pale green and buttery yellow. The mirrors might have appeared out of place but are joined by a small table and basket in the same hue, striking just the right balance of light and dark in the room.

B With a two-story ceiling and curving staircase, this foyer was bound to be fancy. The designer tempered it by using rustic French chairs, choosing seagrass for the stair runner, and draping the table in matelassé.

C Straitlaced Stickley dining chairs and benches combined with this room's pronounced Arts and Crafts architecture could have resulted in a certain stiffness, but with lanterns standing in for a chandelier and the walls upholstered in a charming pear print, it's all perfectly inviting.

D Terra-cotta and patterned tiles, along with a wrought-iron railing, are right at home in this Spanish-Moorish tower, and they combine beautifully with the contemporary blue-and-white bench fabric and textural bamboo blinds. The imported blue glass light fixture ties it all together.

E Clean lines and neutral tones make this eclectic mix of Asian chest, leather-clad director's chairs, and concrete and bottle-glass tabletop hang together. The swirling chandelier acts as a counterpoint.

F Slender antique-style furnishings dressed in chintz and toile, paired with a hand-painted floor screen, bring instant elegance to this brick-walled basement.

G Rattan, bamboo, wrought iron, and a cheerful color palette give this master bedroom an idiosyncratic, flea-market flair.

H British Colonial pieces like this chaise longue tend to dominate a room, so the designer kept the surroundings simple: warm wood floors, white wainscoting, sea-green wall paint, and bamboo blinds.

I Whatever your style, it can be extended to the outdoors, thanks to the range of all-weather furnishings and fabrics now available. These generously proportioned armchairs woven from banana leaves take the same eco-friendly approach as the rest of the home.

color

A Colorful doesn't have to mean bright. This room features pale blues and purples—both cool colors—warmed with touches of russet. Plants add green to the mix.

B Even bright colors—in this case, brilliant yellow—can feel serene when balanced with ample neutrals.

C White, on the other hand, brightens colors. Glossy white walls and awning stripes play up this candy-colored mix.

D This same fabric against light walls would have been cheery; dark, tonal-striped red walls make it exotic.

E Using multiple shades of a color gives a room more visual texture than a single shade.

F Conversely, choosing different colors in the same tonal range is a good way to make sure they'll harmonize. This is especially beneficial when using more than three colors.

G If you're color-shy or just like to keep it simple, pick a single color and deploy it in a variety of ways. The strawberry red of these armchairs repeats in two different patterns—the toile of the throw and spots of the pillows—and in the trim on the sheets and curtains.

H Another sure-fire approach is to use colors that are adjacent on the color wheel, such as red and orange, or blue-green, green, and yellow-green. This bedroom is dressed in shades of blue and purple.

I Complementary colors—those that sit directly across from each other on the color wheel—act as natural foils, and work beautifully together every time. The classic French combination of blue and yellow, as seen on this loggia, is a prime example.

J There's no law that says walls have to be a color and trim has to be white. In this study, white walls get a fresh look from warm grey trim, while dark paint makes the windows—and the view they frame—the focal point of the room.

K In an all-white room, the focus shifts to the mix of materials. The "colors" in this bathroom are marble, chrome, and wood. Keep in mind that in the absence of color, contrast and texture become paramount.

L In an otherwise neutral room, the artwork and objects get to be the stars. This approach also means that changing a room's color scheme is as easy as replacing the accessories.

A

B

C

flooring

A Wood floors add warmth and character to any room, but reclaimed wood planks in random widths—like those in this entryway—bring the added quality of age.

B A floor of large stone tile, laid on the diagonal, is inherently elegant. The designer of this grand foyer toned it down by using humble fabrics and rustic furniture, and, in the same vein, chose a pockmarked java-stone for the floor instead of a fancier marble.

C Intricate geometric patterns, such as this intriguing two-tone "basketweave," once involved painstaking—and thus expensive—installation. They now come prearranged on twelve-inch squares that lie together to form a seamless pattern. So while they may cost more than plain tiles, the installation no longer does.

D, E, F Inlays add interest to any floor, whether wood laid in tile, wood in wood, or tile in tile. Inlays can be used as borders or to create any kind of pattern you might dream up. Here wood strips form a large diagonal pattern with concrete tiles, patterned wood forms a border in a dark wood floor, and glass mosaic tiles form a grid among limestone squares.

G A large rectangular inlay gives the impression of a rug. Here a slate mosaic, bordered in larger slate tiles, contrasts nicely with the light wood floor surrounding it. The slate repeats on the stair risers down the hall.

H In this entryway, dark wood set into lighter wood has the same effect.

I Tile "rugs" can also be custom-painted or bought as kits, complete with borders and sometimes even tile "fringe." This one was painted to look like an antique kilim.

J Patterned tiles bring color and flair to a space. These set a Moroccan tone in a tower sitting room.

K One of the biggest tile trends of the moment is river rock. Carefully chosen and mounted on mesh squares, it is installed just like any other tile. It is a bit pricier than the average tile so is best used in smaller spaces, such as this wine room, where a little bit can make a big impact.

L These multi-hued concrete tiles continue from the patio right into the house. That continuity of the floor surfaces adds to the indoor-outdoor feel of the home.

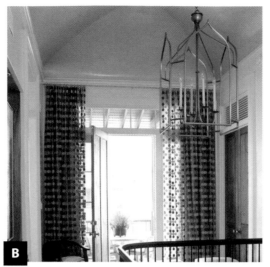

ceilings

A   Glossy white paint offers a surprise on a ceiling—which would traditionally take a flat paint—and adds a gleaming effect to this sun-filled kitchen.

B   Pearly grey paint combines with the dome of this beach house's hall to make it look just like the inside of a seashell.

C   Blue is a popular color for bedrooms because it's considered to be soothing. Continuing the blue of these walls on the ceiling makes the room that much more cocoon-like.

D   The design concept for this sitting room was to cover every surface in the same pale green toile print, creating a sort of wonderland. Including the ceiling makes it work.

E   Decorative wood beams transform a plain white ceiling and combine with the reclaimed wood floors to give this renovated home a sense of age.

F   This timbered oak ceiling runs through the home's living room and kitchen, tying the spaces together despite their differing approaches. The living room's traditional furnishings (page 51) combine with the ceiling in a display of Old World elegance, whereas the rusticity of the ceiling is a striking counterpoint to the sleek, contemporary kitchen.

G, H   The coffered ceiling can be interpreted any number of ways to complement any number of settings. Here a ceiling of wide, white coffers dresses up a casual living room, while a thatched version, with accompanying ceiling fan, lends natural texture to a British Colonial guest room.

I   This exposed pine ceiling, somewhere between coffers and rafters, plays off the room's paneling and contrasts nicely with the darker rattan of the furnishings.

J   Exposed rafters and beams amplify the volume of this great room but also lend it warmth.

K   Whitewashed rafters instantly set an island tone. This designer played up the look with a ceiling fan, wicker furnishings, and other tropical touches.

L   Painted the traditional porch-ceiling blue, exposed rafters take on a Southern flavor and add charm to this basic bathroom.

D

E

F

G

H

I

K

L

details make the difference

wall treatments

A Wide stripes are a popular trick for adding character to a plain wall. This one takes a subtle approach, with stripes of a single color in matte and gloss finishes.

B Think beyond paint and paper: If there's a fabric you love, consider having the walls upholstered in it, for a softer effect. This pear print was also used for window treatments in the adjacent kitchen.

C Paneling is back in vogue. It lends warmth and texture to a room—particularly when the surface is as intriguing as the pecky cypress of this sitting room.

D In this alternative take on paneling, wood strips have been applied to the wall in a decorative pattern, then painted to match. The pattern plays off the railing and the tansu-style cabinets built into the stairs.

E The paneling of this dining room was hand-painted to mimic traditional scenic wallpaper, giving the room its elegant ambiance.

F For a unique look, these walls were coated with brown kraft paper from the office supply, applied with wheat paste.

G For subtle interest in this neutral bedroom, squares of grasscloth in two different shades were applied to the wall in a checkerboard pattern.

H A paneled niche makes it seem as if this mosaic-tiled wall is floating in front of a wooden one. A shadow line in the recess furthers the effect.

I Tile is unnecessary in a powder room, where the walls are not likely to get wet, which makes these brilliant blue walls that much more surprising and entrancing—especially as glimpsed through the arched doorway.

J Any stone available as counter slabs can also be had in tile form—and is often drastically cheaper per square foot. Here the honed granite from the kitchen's perimeter counters repeats as a backsplash.

K When using tile in an oversize wallpaper pattern like this one—or any striking tile, for that matter—why not go ahead and tile the whole wall?

L A tile backsplash makes as much sense in an outdoor kitchen as indoors. This one uses large ceramic tiles in earthy colors.

window treatments

A A white roller blind in a white room is the most minimal of window treatments, all but disappearing when it's rolled up. That can be desirable with a large, attractive window or great view that you don't want to lose, or in a spot where glare and privacy are only occasionally factors.

B Café curtains are a good solution where full-length curtains are either impossible or impractical, or where the upper part of the window—and the view—are especially appealing. This extra-short version consists of a single panel of fabric, with the rod threaded through a series of grommets.

C Classic window-length curtains, with a ruffled valance, are perfectly suited to this sunny yellow laundry room. The combination makes the room feel as if it's straight out of the 1950s.

D Café curtains aren't the only way to leave the upper reaches of windows open; blinds—such as these in bamboo—can also be hung lower in the frame. This works best with blinds that have a plain upper edge rather than a flap or valance built in.

E A loose roman shade makes these French doors feel more window-like and adds another note of softness to the cozily upholstered room.

F Roman shades come in a variety of styles and can be fashioned from any fabric to complement any room. Here green horizontal stripes play off the wider, paler stripes of the surrounding walls.

G, H Blinds and shades not only make a fresher-looking companion to drapes than old-fashioned sheers, they don't permanently obscure the windows. Roman shades offer a second layer of color or pattern, while wood blinds provide texture and allow for the greatest control of light and privacy. With any drapes, hanging the rod higher than the top of the window makes for longer drapery, creating additional height in the room.

I Bowed rods create a unique effect, lending extra volume to the flat planes of the windows. In this bedroom, the same rod and fabric were used to create a pseudo-canopy above the headboard.

upholstery

A Mix-and-match piping takes colorful upholstery one step further. The contrasting edging on the chair and ottoman also plays up the forms by making the furniture's outlines more distinct.

B An upholstered ottoman is a welcome companion to any chair, but a large round one such as this can float in a room and serve a variety of purposes—from extra seating to an occasional table.

C Seating isn't the only thing that can be upholstered. A leather-covered cube, with decorative brass nailheads, makes a chic end table.

D, E Curvy or straight, button-tufted or contrast-edged, contemporary or traditional, an upholstered headboard is as sensible as it is appealing. Create your own headboard with plywood, batting, and upholstery fabric, or have an upholsterer copy one from a photo.

F A relatively simple alternative to an upholstered headboard is to pad, upholster, and frame the patch of wall behind the bed. This designer also upholstered the spaces beside the bed, playing up the way the bed is set into the wall of windows.

G, H Who says you have to pick just one fabric per chair? A contrasting seat and back add character to this dining chair, while the armchairs' coordinating patterns outside and inside give them a casual air.

I Slipcovers are especially practical for dining chairs since they're easy to clean or replace. To dress up a simple wood chair, consider a skirted slipcover.

J An upholstered floor screen makes a statement in any setting. This one is used to define a space rather than divide it—helping to turn a console table into a chic makeshift bar in this screened porch.

K Major advances in outdoor fabric technology have led to an explosion of available patterns and colors. Now outdoor rooms can be every bit as stylish and comfortable as those indoors.

L Whether a box, a bench, or a low stone wall like this one, any surface can become instant seating with the addition of an upholstered cushion.

D

E

F

G

H

I

K

L

the art of display

A Objects work best together when they share a trait. This collection features vases in both glass and pottery, all in gourd shapes.

B The same goes for this display of veined stone—the tabletop, lamp base, and figurine—and wood pieces, grouped into like sets. The frame on the wall shares traits of both.

C Grouping and simplicity are fundamental in keeping open shelving from looking messy. In addition to choosing simple glassware and neutral pottery, this designer stashed wine bottles in bamboo cages, which are in keeping with the room's beachy decor.

D On a high shelf running around the perimeter of this breakfast nook, colorful, vintage glass bottles seem like they could have washed up on the shore outside.

E, F Paintings and photography aren't the only things that can be hung on walls. Here freeform glass bowls in a hallway and African headdresses above a desk make for especially intriguing displays.

G, H Just about everything benefits from being hung in multiples. Witness these fish-eye mirrors and soft botanical prints: both would have had less impact hung solo.

I Three-dimensional objects can also be hung in deep frames, shadow box–style. Again, these dried garlands were hung as a group to up their impact and interest.

J The designer of this room made creative use of the molding along the top of the wainscoting: She hung a painting and collection of plates to look as if they're propped on the ledge. The height of the wainscoting makes it work.

K Furnishings and wall hangings can often feel like exactly that: a group of furnishings with a group of wall hangings floating above it. To make everything cohere, this mirror and botanical prints were hung close together and low to the dresser.

L Mantels and the wall space above them are classic spots for displaying cherished art and objects, but the mouth of the fireplace is often a missed opportunity. This one contains a porcelain piece that matches those on and above the mantel.

finishing touches

A Add flair to any drapery by considering the edges. Contrasting fabric is a simple way to add color and definition, but the black bell fringe chosen for the drapery on the beds of this girl's room adds texture and a sort of whimsical glamour.

B Rather than leaving the space over the fireplace open for a painting, this designer brought quirky pattern and texture to the room by fashioning a "wall hanging" out of the same paneling used on the wall, bringing a finished feeling to the room before it was even furnished.

C A simple thing like updating a lampshade can make a world of difference. Taking over for the standard-issue white shade, this woven raffia shade visually links the glossy white bedside table and the textural bamboo bed it's partnered with.

D Even a bathroom—perhaps especially a bathroom—benefits from a beautiful painting and the refinement of such things as brass sconces and fresh flowers.

E Decorative table legs applied to the four corners of this island are an amusing acknowledgment that the island has widely displaced the kitchen table of yesteryear.

F Another whimsical touch: a galvanized bucket and stool standing in for the sink in the powder room of this laid-back fishing camp.

G The doorway to this basement surf-themed lounge and pool room—inset with panels of resin and seashells—sets the expectation for what's to come.

H Rugs, throw pillows, and well-positioned tables make a room more comfortable and more usable. This goes double outdoors. Here seagrass matting and neutral fabrics, combined with long-wearing teak furniture, set a calm tone on a balcony overlooking sand and surf.

I For the entrance to this partially enclosed cabana under the home's deck, the designer chose not just any screen door but one with a charming fish pattern.

storage

A For an effective pantry, organization is key. This closet-size space benefits from a mix of open shelving, drawers—some with acrylic fronts—and vertical dividers for platters. All contribute to easily finding what one needs.

B Opposite the kitchen and just inside the back door, the space under these stairs has been converted to open shelving— keeping shoes and gear from accumulating on the hall floor.

C Inside formal, narrow, or high-traffic entrances, it's preferable for rain shoes and other miscellany to be kept out of sight. This ingenious cabinet has mesh doors, which allow damp items to air out.

D Floor space for bookshelves is almost always in short supply. Building them into the walls on the stair landing, as this designer did, makes use of otherwise wasted space.

E Likewise, cabinets built into the doorways at intervals along this hallway add up to quite a lot of additional storage space without imposing on the rooms.

F In a kitchen, the choice between cabinetry and windows can be a difficult one. Here shelf brackets were mounted on the window frame, allowing for both sunlight and storage.

G The top of most window seats lifts up to reveal a storage cavity. This seat takes a different approach, concealing file drawers under its upholstered bench.

H What looks like built-in cabinets beside this fireplace is actually a cleverly designed door, which opens to reveal a hidden storage vault.

I For extra seating that also conceals fresh pool towels, this loggia was furnished with an antique hall bench with the characteristic hinged seat.

J Vintage cubby units were stacked in the corner of this exercise room for storing a variety of gear and supplies.

K Space was carved out in this master suite for a "to-go area," with cabinets for luggage, a counter for folding and getting organized, and a corkboard for itineraries and notes.

L Better than a buffet, a wall of cabinetry in this dining room stores a wealth of dishes, silver, and table linens. The counter-top functions as a bar or serving surface; the mirror keeps the room feeling open.

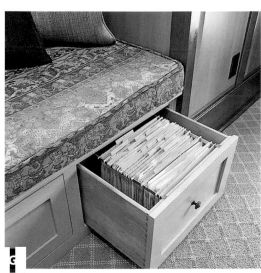

bonus space

A This closet-size niche between the kitchen and dining room became invaluable when converted to a small workstation geared toward menu-planning and other household business.

B A window seat tucked into a niche and shelving sunk into the wall turn this landing into a reading nook. The warm red wall emphasizes the seat and frames the desert view.

C A full wall of open shelving above shallow cabinets makes this hallway a combination library, gallery, and storage room. The navy blue behind the shelves is a dramatic backdrop for the objects upon them. The transom above the bedroom door allows extra light into the hallway.

D Improving on the traditional swing, this rear porch has a hanging full-size bed. As simple as a platform suspended from heavy-duty chains, it effectively gives the homeowners an extra bedroom, as well as a premium spot for napping.

E This landing is wide enough to host a pair of loveseats, a TV cabinet stocked with video and board games, and an expandable game table, making it a great place for kids to convene while the grown-ups entertain downstairs, or for the whole family to get together for a movie or game of Monopoly.

F Rather than wasting the space behind the knee wall, or using it for storage, it was left open to the little girl's room and decorated as a playhouse, complete with door, windows, furnishings, and trompe l'oeil landscaping.

G A storage wall with a built-in murphy bed means this room can function as a guest room when needed, while being available for other uses—a home office or exercise room— in the meantime.

H There was no game room in the floor plan of this Southern California home, so the designer took to the outdoors— converting a patch of patio into a recreation room, with a pool table tucked under an arbor.

I Plenty of headroom under this beach home's deck inspired the designers to erect partial walls and created a cabana, complete with lounge chairs and a hot tub.

smart homes

A "Modern appliances" no longer means just a microwave and dishwasher. Warming drawers and wine fridges are now expanding the kitchen's capabilities.

B This is the bathroom of the future. The shower is programmable: Each person can set his or her showerhead position and water temperature preferences and retrieve them with the touch of a button. The bathroom windows are also high-tech, switching from clear to translucent with the flip of a switch, for a choice between a view and privacy.

C The dumbwaiter fell out of fashion long ago, but in this home it has been reinterpreted as the natural companion for the laundry chute. No more hauling laundry down or up.

D Central vacuum systems are effective and efficient, mainly because they eliminate the need to store and haul around a clunky conventional machine. In this kitchen, a toe kick in the baseboard feeds directly into the system, making the dustpan equally obsolete.

E One of life's simplest luxuries is a dry, warm towel. This spa bathroom's towel-warmer—with its discreet glass rod—ensures exactly that.

F The blinds in this beachfront bedroom are not just UV-blocking—protecting the room's residents and contents from the sun's damaging rays—they are remote-controlled, so one needn't get out of bed to let in the sunrise.

G An ingenious shade system was created for this arbor. Shade cloth is fitted with dowels and hung on a rigging, so it can be easily pulled back for the desired mix of sun and shade.

H Motorized, retractable screens give these homeowners the option of switching back and forth between an open porch and screened.

I Synthetic materials—from porch posts and decking to "wicker" furniture—mean everything holds up better to the weather.

design and photo credits

The homes shown throughout this book were developed and photographed by the following teams:

ABBERLEY LANE
Southern Living

Interior Design: Hansen & Associates Interiors; Cullen Albright, Joci Firth • Architecture: John Tee • Construction: Hallmark Homes • Photography by Jean Allsopp, Laurey W. Glenn • Seen on pages 5 right, 125 bottom left and bottom right, 235 F

ALABAMA FITHOUSE
Cooking Light

Interior Design: Ellyn Enslen Richey Designs • Architecture: Dungan-Nequette Architects; Jeff Dungan • Construction: Lifescape Builders • Photography by John O'Hagan • Seen on pages 4 top right, 232 C, 245 J, 248 C

BIRMINGHAM SHOWHOUSE
Southern Accents

Interior Design: Mary Evelyn McKee Interiors; Mary Evelyn McKee, Mallory Wadley Rushing • Architecture: Henry Sprott Long & Associates; Jeanette Wilson, Henry Long Jr., Andy Troncalli, Chilton Porter, Ray A. White, Catherine Blair, Craig L. Hennecy, Norman Nix, Ann Best, Richard Sprague • Construction: Francis A. Bryant & Sons • Photography by Jeff McNamara • Seen on pages 28–29, 50–55, 126–127, 136, 146–149, 166–169, 188–189, 204–205, 230 C, 233 F, 239 J, 242 A, 243 D

CALIFORNIA IDEA HOUSE
Sunset

Interior Design: Stone-Wood Design, Inc.; Janice Stone Thomas • Architecture: Kevin Patrick O'Brien Architects • Construction: Kensington Homes, Inc. • Photography by David Wakely • Seen on pages 245 G, 245 H

COOL AND CONTEMPORARY
IDEA HOUSE
Sunset

Interior Design: Bethe Cohen Design Associates • Construction: De Mattei Construction • Photography by Muffy Kibbey • Seen on pages 5 left, 111 left, 161 middle, 207 bottom right, 227 E, 235 D

DALLAS SHOWHOUSE
Southern Accents

Interior Design: Cathy Kincaid Interiors; Cathy Kincaid, Maggie Kincaid, Betsy Massey, Charles Birdsong, Anne Barcus, Ladye Kay Allen • Architecture: Fusch-Serold & Partners; Robbie Fusch, Alfredo Levy • Construction: Bob Thompson Homes • Photography by Antoine Bootz, Jeff McNamara • Seen on pages 82–85, 116–117, 207 middle left, 212–213, 226 B, 227 F, 228 A, 229 D, 229 I, 230 B, 233 D, 236 C, 237 I, 239 D, 239 H, 241 K, 241 L, 245 I

EAST BEACH HIDEAWAY
Coastal Living

Interior Design: T.S. Hudson Interiors; Linda Woodrum • Architecture: Chuck Dietsche • Photography by John O'Hagan • Seen on pages 156–157

EMERSON HILL
Southern Living

Interior Design: Woodvale Interiors; Connie Smith Howard, Jessica Gilmore • Architecture: Ben Patterson • Construction: Frank Stone & Son Construction Co. • Photography by Van Chaplin • Seen on pages 100–101, 110, 218–219

ENGLISH RESTORATION
Southern Accents

Architecture and Interior Design: Bill Ingram Architect; Bill Ingram, Marie Blackwell, Darla Davis • Construction: Francis A. Bryant & Sons • Photography by Tria Giovan, Howard L. Puckett • Seen on pages 18–19, 32–39, 98–99, 158, 216–217, 228 B, 230 A, 231 D, 233 E, 234 C, 237 E, 241 G

FAMILY REUNION
Coastal Living

Interior Design: T.S. Hudson Interiors; Linda Woodrum • Architecture: George Graves • Photography by Deborah Whitlaw • Seen on pages 26–27, 86–87, 233 I, 249 F

GEORGIA FITHOUSE
Cooking Light

Interior Design: Carter Kay Interiors • Architecture: Caldwell-Cline Architects and Designers, Inc. • Construction: Nick C. Schiltz, Inc. • Photography by John O'Hagan • Seen on pages 111 right, 137 left, 249 D

GREYWELL COTTAGE

Southern Living

Interior Design: J. Edwards Interiors •
Architecture: Frusterio & Associates, Inc. •
Construction: Buchanan Custom Homes •
Photography by Jean Allsopp • Seen on
page 135

HARROD'S CREEK

Southern Living

Interior Design: CGA Interiors; Debbi
Wayman • Architecture: Cornerstone Group
Architects; Mark Carlson, Bob Wetmore •
Construction: Michael Deane Homes •
Photography by John O'Hagan • Seen
on pages 24–25, 96–97, 229 F, 231 K

HIGHLANDS COVE SHOWHOUSE

Southern Accents

Interior Design: Phillip Sides Interior
Design; Phillip Sides, Jan Cowart, Wanda
Fussell, Mary Stephens, Chris Brown,
Caroline Sain, Lynda White, Michael
Bohannon • Architecture: Harrison Design
Associates • Construction: Southeastern
Construction & Mgt. • Photography by Tria
Giovan • Seen on pages 4 left, 10–13, 68–73,
120–121, 162–165, 170–175, 207 top right,
220, 226 C, 234 B, 238 B, 239 L, 240 B, 245 E

INNOVATION HOUSE

Sunset

Interior Design: McDonald & Moore •
Architecture: Dahlin Group Architecture
and Planning • Construction: De Mattei
Construction • Photography by Thomas J.
Story • Seen on pages 7, 229 L, 231 L, 235 L,
236 A, 247 G, 248 B, 249 E

KINSLEY PLACE

Southern Living

Interior Design: Brooks Interior Design;
Donna Brooks, Shona Binkowski •
Architecture: Looney Ricks Kiss Architects;
Carson Looney, Mark Jones, Chris Haley •
Construction: The St. Joe Company •
Photography by Laurey W. Glenn • Seen
on pages 92–95, 134, 243 E, 244 B, 249 H

LIVE OAK COTTAGE

Southern Living

Interior Design: Mary E. Solomon Interiors •
Architecture: Looney Ricks Kiss Architects;
Carson Looney, David Kenoyer • Construction: The St. Joe Company • Photography
by Van Chaplin • Seen on pages 108–109,
239 I, 245 K

NEWBERRY PARK

Southern Living

Interior Design: Steiner + Schelfe Design,
LLC • Architecture: Allison Ramsey
Architects; Bill Allison, Steve Hand •
Construction: Dixon/Kirby & Company,
Inc. • Photography by Jean Allsopp •
Seen on pages 112, 236 B, 245 F, 247 D

NEW YORK IDEA HOME

Cottage Living

Interior Design: Steven Gambrel •
Architecture: Historical Concepts; Jim
Strickland, Joshua Roland, Domenick
Treschitta, Terry Pylant • Construction:
Windward Builders, LLC • Photography
by Tria Giovan • Seen on pages 4 bottom
right, 40–45, 106–107, 118–119, 130, 150–151,
160, 222–223, 228 C, 229 J, 232 A, 238 A, 239 E,
240 C, 241 D, 242 C, 245 D

OLD DOMINION SHOWHOUSE

Southern Accents

Interior Design: David H. Mitchell Design;
David H. Mitchell, Kristi Popernack •
Architecture: Harrison Design Associates;
Bill Harrison, Bulent Baydar, Dietrich Logan,
John Albanese, Greg Palmer • Construction:
Artisan Builders • Photography by Tria
Giovan • Seen on pages 1, 62–67, 122–123,
133, 186–187, 190–191, 225, 229 E, 235 E,
235 J, 239 K, 240 A, 241 H, 241 I

ORANGE COUNTY IDEA HOUSE

Sunset

Interior Design: Annie Speck Interior
Designs • Architecture: Eric Trabert &
Associates • Construction: Mulvaney & Co.
• Photography by Thomas J. Story • Seen
on pages 88–89, 104–105, 114–115, 138, 194,
229 H, 231 E, 231 F, 233 G, 243 G, 245 L

PALM GARDEN RETREAT

Coastal Living

Interior Design: Lovelace Interiors; Susan
Lovelace, Debbie Faulkner, Connie Simpson
• Architecture: Cooper Johnson Smith;
Mike Willis, Don Cooper, Jennifer Garcia •
Construction: Bayfair • Photography by
Jean Allsopp • Seen on pages 3, 22–23,
208–209, 226 A, 227 H, 229 K, 233 H, 247 E

PALO ALTO IDEA HOUSE

Sunset

Interior Design: Pamela Pennington
Studios • Architecture: C. David Robinson
Architects; Dahlin Group (Consultant) •
Construction: SummerHill Homes •
Photography by Muffy Kibbey • Seen
on page 231 H

PARKVIEW

Southern Living

Interior Design: Nevin Interior Design •
Architecture: Historical Concepts;
Terry Pylant, Kelly Andrews Scibona, Jim
Strickland, Ryan Yurcaba • Construction:
Whitehall Homes • Photography by Ralph
Anderson • Seen on pages 128–129, 206,
239 F, 244 C, 246 C

PINE RIDGE FARM

The Progressive Farmer

Interior Design: Parker Furniture •
Architecture: Donald Gardner Architects,
Inc. • Construction: McLendon Hills
Construction • Photography by John
O'Hagan, Rob Lagerstrom • Seen on
page 207 middle right

ROSEMARY BEACH SHOWHOUSE

Southern Accents

Interior Design: Phillip Sides Interior
Design; Phillip Sides, Stacey Jordan,
Wanda Fussell, Mary Stephens, Rob
Sowell, Amanda Morgan • Architecture:
Arc Design Atlanta, Inc.; Michelle Castaner,
Jack Richards, Lew Oliver • Construction:
New Creation Builders, Inc. • Photography
by Tria Giovan • Seen on pages 2, 8, 46–49,
124, 140–143, 152–153, 161 bottom, 180–185,
202–203, 207 top left, 232 B, 233 J, 235 H,
235 I, 237 F, 237 G, 237 H, 238 C, 241 E, 242 B,
243 H

SALADO VIEW

Southern Living

Interior Design: David Collum Interiors;
David Collum, Mary Collum, Stephanie
Latham • Architecture: New Home Solutions; Greg Setzer • Construction: Broadway
5 Homes • Photography by Van Chaplin •
Seen on pages 125 top left and top right,
239 G

SAND MOUNTAIN COTTAGE

The Progressive Farmer

Interior Design: Holcombe Associates •
Architecture: John Tee • Construction:
DesignMark • Photography by John
O'Hagan, Mary Margaret Chambliss,
Rob Lagerstrom • Seen on page 248 A

SHIPSHAPE COTTAGE

Coastal Living

Interior Design: Linda Woodrum •
Architecture: Summerour and Associates
Architects; Thad Truett, Keith Summerour •
Construction: Pipe Construction Company
• Photography by Jean Allsopp, Rex Perry •
Seen on pages 78–81, 90, 229 G, 233 K, 233 L,
243 I, 247 I

SOUTHERN CALIFORNIA IDEA HOUSE

Sunset

Interior Design: Artistic Environments •
Architecture: David George & Associates;
Architopia • Construction: HyMax Building
Corp. • Photography by Lisa Romerein •
Seen on pages 30–31, 137 right, 214–215,
227 D, 231 I, 231 J, 234 A, 235 K, 246 A

SOUTHWEST IDEA HOUSE

Sunset

Interior Design: Tamm Jasper Interiors •
Architecture: Dale Gardon Design •
Construction: Salcito Custom Homes •
Photography by Thomas J. Story • Seen
on pages 102–103, 161 top, 207 bottom left,
244 A, 246 B, 247 H, 249 G

**TENNESSEE IDEA HOUSE
& FARMSTEAD**

The Progressive Farmer

Interior Design: G. Kelly Interiors •
Architecture: Looney Ricks Kiss Architects •
Construction: Hatcliff Construction •
Photography by Rob Lagerstrom, John
O'Hagan • Seen on page 131 right

TEXAS FITHOUSE

Cooking Light

Interior Design: Laura Britt Design •
Architecture: BBG Architects •
Construction: Spanish Oaks Master
Builder • Photography by Tria Giovan •
Seen on pages 74–77, 227 I, 241 F

TIDEWATER LANDING

Coastal Living

Interior Design: Lovelace Interiors; Susan
Lovelace, Allyson Jones, Debbie Faulkner •
Architecture: Folck West + Savage; Gerrie
King West • Construction: J.M. Sykes, Inc. •
Photography by Jean Allsopp, Harry Taylor •
Seen on pages 20–21, 56–61, 144–145, 154–
155, 176–179, 210–211, 249 I

WALKER'S BLUFF

Southern Living

Interior Design: Macci Designs, Inc. •
Architecture: Gary/Ragsdale, Inc. • Construction: Marlowe Homes • Photography
by Jean Allsopp, Van Chaplin • Seen on
pages 132, 241 J, 247 F

WARM AND COLORFUL IDEA HOUSE

Sunset

Interior Design: Ann Bertelsen, Leanne
Holder • Construction: De Mattei
Construction • Photography by Muffy
Kibbey • Seen on pages 192–193, 231 G,
235 G

WEST BAY LANDING

Southern Living

Interior Design: Lovelace Interiors; Susan
Lovelace, Patricia Kramer • Architecture:
Lake/Flato Architects, Inc.; Ted Flato, Craig
McMahon, Jonathan Card • Construction:
Paul Thrasher Construction • Photography
by Jean Allsopp • Seen on pages 14–17,
125 middle left and middle right, 131 left,
196–201, 227 G, 243 F